COUNT

COUNT

Valerie Martínez

THE UNIVERSITY OF
ARIZONA PRESS
TUCSON

The University of Arizona Press
www.uapress.arizona.edu

ISBN-13: 978-0-8165-4219-2 (paperback)

Cover design by Leigh McDonald
Cover art: *River Oats Volume One* by Basia Irland
Designed and typeset by Leigh McDonald in Acie WF (display) and Adobe Jenson Pro 11/14

Publication of this book is made possible in part by the proceeds of a permanent endowment created with the assistance of a Challenge Grant from the National Endowment for the Humanities, a federal agency.

Library of Congress Cataloging-in-Publication Data
Names: Martínez, Valerie, 1961– author.
Title: Count / Valerie Martínez.
Other titles: Camino del sol.
Description: Tucson : University of Arizona Press, 2021. | Series: Camino del sol: a Latinx
    literary series
Identifiers: LCCN 2020051185 | ISBN 9780816542192 (paperback)
Subjects: LCSH: Nature—Effect of human beings on—Poetry. | Narrative poetry, American. |
    LCGFT: Narrative poetry. | Ecopoetry.
Classification: LCC PS3563.A73345 C68 2021 | DDC 811/.54—dc23
LC record available at https://lccn.loc.gov/2020051185

Printed in the United States of America
♾ This paper meets the requirements of ANSI/NISO Z39.48-1992 (Permanence of Paper).

For Peter, Alexandra, Sierra, Niall, Serafina,

Río, José Ramón III, and Annelisa—

as we try to live on the edge of great balance,

for you, for yours, for theirs

FOREWORD

I CANNOT THINK OF A TIMELIER book than *Count*. And I wouldn't trust such a book from a poet who's not as attuned as Valerie Martínez to the urgencies of environmental issues and their inextricable bond to social justice. Martínez has shaped a poetics that weaves the ecological with the mythical with the personal. She scaffolds story with the language of the scientific community, the knowledge of the land's indigenous peoples, and the insights of a socially conscious speaker.

This book-length poem's inventory of damage underscores the incompatibility of nature and the industrial world, and it indicts the colonial and capitalist greed that continues to silence reason and reconciliation. Martínez beseeches us to pay attention, to grapple with what it means to see:

> For three consecutive nights I dream we are stick figures
> in a giant earth tome: book of mudslides, book of super-
>
> storms, book of drought-devastated fields inside which
> we tumble like the drawings at Puako—right side up,
>
> sideways, flipped. Are we singing? Are we dancing?
> Are we waving frantically in distress?

One of the most startling movements in Martínez's work is how an image or a memory opens like a porthole, transporting the speaker to another surprising landscape. In one poem, for example, a scar on a man's thigh—the result of a boyish act of carelessness—connects to a piece of performance art filmed on the shores of Israel, in which a woman spins a barbed-wire Hula-Hoop on her bare midriff as a statement about borders and the violence they inflict upon the body. With this juxtaposition of times and locations, Martínez instigates a whirlpool of critical thinking about the politics of gender and power, of relationship to history (personal and global), and of purpose and intent.

Count is not only invested in an intellectual journey, however; an emotional one is inevitable as the poems echo and recall Martínez's charged imagery. The previous poem, for example, reaches back to an earlier one about the speaker's encounter with a manatee in a bay whose natural components date back millions of years and exist in the present only by enduring an unnatural invasion of motorboats and plastic waste. The manatee, like its kin, "bears a unique pattern of scars // recognizable to researchers, one by one telling / its tales of brutal encounters with humans." Then is joined to now as here to there.

Interconnectedness means everyone bears responsibility, since no one will remain unaffected by the consequences of human folly, such as global warming, rising sea levels, and the certainty of climate change immigration. But Martínez doesn't proselytize from the soapbox. A formidable stylist, she uses surprising leaps and exquisite lyricism to craft such furious portraits:

> . . . Outside the leafy banyans drip
> their aerial branches like lions' tails, and the houses keep
>
> shining on—mango, avocado, tangerine—cheerful amnesiacs,
> while a time lapse depicts shrinking ice sheets, disappearing

beachfronts, and the room is so fraught with quiet I stifle
the urge to mumble and cough.

Count is an extraordinary book-length poem that has arrived to
hold us accountable. Those of us who are witnessing the present
moment and who maintain inaction, indifference, or mere residence
in industrial nations are complicit in the destruction of the world's
resources and in the extinction and endangerment of precious flora
and fauna. *Count* is counting the days to our critical awakening or
to our annihilation. *Count* is counting on us to follow the right path.

—*Rigoberto González*
Camino del Sol Series Editor

ACKNOWLEDGMENTS

EXCERPTS FROM COUNT HAVE BEEN PUBLISHED, sometimes in earlier versions, in the following publications:

Duke City Fix
saltfront
Taos Journal of Poetry and Art
The American Scholar

COUNT

I

Saturday afternoon with Serafina in the back seat, tethered
to iPhone, singing somewhere between off-key and tune,

we approach the girl on the median, a handwritten sign:
CAR WASH U NO U WANT ONE. Eyelet top, short-

shorts, black bra peeking through, long line of cars, men
folded over windows flipping U-turns into a parking lot,

where the football team kicks back in lawn chairs, where
more girls in cutoffs and bikini tops soap up sedans, pickups,

and the water, water, water sliding off hubcaps, pooling
on asphalt, pouring endlessly into storm drains. I watch

Fina, almost 13, turn her head till her neck can no longer
twist and I am dumbstruck for once—male gaze, division

of labor, critical drought. She eyes me, expectant. Instead
I go deep in, remember the Thornicroft's giraffe strangely

isolated from the herd, bending to her dead calf—
splaying, standing, splaying again. I say nothing.

2

Near the La Luz trailhead, 7,032 feet, we sidestep a thicket—
Cylindropuntia imbricata. Drought tolerant, difficult to kill,

stippled with bees and magenta blooms, the spaces it fills
in the shadows of colossal boulders. We hike up, southeast,

watch a lip of brown creep up the foothills, inch by inch,
below which the green world disappears. It's hard

not to think *akin, continuous, north and south*—Greenland
with its radical ice melt, the advance of the Atacama Desert—

when I hear it: a brimming, a lapping, a sequence of little roars.

3

Let us go now, you and I, to the water—to the girl
who stands alone at the sea. The ocean is the color

of milk and green-gray leaves. It's cold, overcast;
I can see the goose bumps on her legs. She happens

to wear white; she must be 7 or 8. The girl
goes to the water—I see her during the day, at night,

when looking straight on in that highway-drive
hypnotic state. She reminds me of my nieces,

the infants they were, the plastic tubs and soapy water,
the sounds they made, gurgling while they were bathed.

4

Once upon a time the ground upon which we stand
was merely a skin over the ocean. The god Pirman

poked it and flooded the land. Only 2 survived,
a woman and a man, sealed inside a ship of pulai wood.

As the waters receded they nibbled their way outside,
dropped into a field of rhododendrons. Alone,

they bemoaned the absence of children. Later,
the woman gave birth from the flesh of her calves,

from which we are all descended.

5

Water stressed, the ice plant closes its stomata in daylight,
curbing evapotranspiration, opens them at night to absorb

more carbon dioxide. Phenotypic plasticity is the ability
of an organism to adapt to a rapidly changing environment.

Lettuce produces more phytochemicals, the intertidal crab
remakes its gills, *Arabidopsis* undergoes dramatic trans-

scriptomic reprogramming. And so I walk away, euphoric,
from the Lomas Tramway public library, unzip my jacket

in the unseasonably hot October wind, imagining
Mesembryanthemum at the end of a long, hallucinogenic

twilight, waking brightly into morning.

6

Each month for two years I let Dr. Samanen sink me deep
into hypnosis, her *19, 18, 17, 16* like the downward count

at the start of old movies, and in there I saw a series
of creatures—tadpole, she-elephant, hippo, the double-

humped camel inside which my infant-self curled up
peacefully. I'd leave her office without the capacity

for speech, as if language were no longer inherent, as if
the slow upward count lifting me back into consciousness

was incomplete and I lingered in some feral place
where the outline of my body blurred, and the space

between me and my creatures no longer existed.

7

On the asphalt path at Shark Valley, the Tarzan screech
of a limpkin knocks me back into midday, bicycling

through muggy air, and I resume the alligator count—
28, 29, 30, 31—basking at path side or half-submerged

in the slough. The year I bounce between high desert
and wetlands, deeply incised riverbeds and this 15-mile

loop seeming to float on water. I swerve from the carapace
of an apple snail, *Pomacea canaliculata*, see a dozen more

scattered on saw grass, sedge sitting precariously atop
a vanishing layer of Everglades peat. I am far from home,

here, where water hovers in all its forms, a behemoth
pulsing through me, breath and breath, like Samoan Octopus,

children Fire and Water locked in epic battle, triggering
the rise of a boundless sea, yet another tale of the deluge

wiping the slate clean.

8

In the sixties in the backyard of the San Ildefonso house
we ran the spigot for hours, full blast, let go the garden hose

to watch it corkscrew and dance, tried to catch it, tame it,
pin it under our soaked shoes. High desert water ran wild

those hot summers—sheen on the shoulders, cool shine.
Twisting our soaked heads, letting the drops fly.

Bill Viola's slow-motion video, *The Raft*, begins simply—
strangers wait for a bus or train, yawning, checking the time.

Water blasts into the frame right and left—leaden tsunami,
fog, impenetrable cloud. All are taken down. The water

recedes and stops, interminably drips from hems, shirt
cuffs, torpid split ends. They labor into consciousness,

lift themselves up, and only then can they reach out,
pull each other up, telling me something about extremity,

something I don't want to know.

9

Hiking into piñon, the mountain fades from green to yellow
to caramel brown—100 million dead trees in the Southwest

alone. The bark beetle thrives on drought, devours the phloem,
starves the scaly trunks. Just one spark—campfire, cigarette—

and a sea of brittle trees bursts wildly into flames. In Giza,
1250 BC, the dung beetle seemed to emerge spontaneously

from its burrow, spurred by a mysterious force, and so
was worshipped as Khepera, "He Who Comes Forth,"

pushing the sun faster on its course. The Egyptians placed
gold scarabs over the hearts of the mummified, inscribed

with a spell from the Book of the Dead: "make no failure
in respect of me before the Master of Balance."

10

Professor Harold Wanless clicks through a series of images:
Florida, Antarctica, a lecture entitled "The Frightening Reality

of Sea Level Rise" for the crush of a standing-room crowd
including the well-heeled and generously-housed residents

of Coral Gables. In the dark we slip into the silence of black
and white, a topography so stark even our paper coffee cups

seem to gush in comparison. Outside the leafy banyans drip
their aerial branches like lions' tails, and the houses keep

shining on—mango, avocado, tangerine—cheerful amnesiacs,
while a time lapse depicts shrinking ice sheets, disappearing

beachfronts, and the room is so fraught with quiet I stifle
the urge to mumble and cough.

II

In anticipation of the great flood, the god Tochopa tucked
his young daughter, Pu-keh-eh, into a piñon trunk

hollowed and packed with nuts, tubers, healing herbs,
hoping she would survive, find another, repopulate

the world. As the waters began to rise he sang and prayed,
held fiercely to the trunk until he, too, and the woodpile

and the houses and the village were subsumed and all
he could do, below in the undertow, was let her go.

12

The girl in white, her small ankles, the gray waves
rising darkly into thunderclouds. The way she backs

and backs away.

13

At Oleta River State Park I leave the trail for a bench,
watch the speedboats and yachts, solitary fishermen

casting their nets. Intermittent blasts of radio hip-hop,
metal, and pop. I count 14 plastic bags embedded

in limestone, hear the bubblings of bay water as it drifts
up and through this shelf of calcium carbonate: coral,

Bryozoa, crinoids, microscopic algae. The fossiliferous
peaks of Texas's Guadalupe Mountains tell us a reef

was there too, in the Permian Period, 280 million
years ago, now 8,700 feet above sea level. A mass

of gray rock shifts. I blink, watch it float, realize
it's no rock but a manatee, my first sighting.

It's late February; they're still here for the winter.
I have seen them only in books and pamphlets, know

they are endangered—floodgates, boat propellers,
monofilament. Each bears a unique pattern of scars

recognizable to researchers, one by one telling
its tales of brutal encounters with humans.

14

My brother James has a nasty scar on his upper right thigh,
Frankenstein zip—accidental fall into glass, frantic drive

to the ER. Thirty years later he revealed the lie: no,
it was self-inflicted, swinging broken bottles back and forth

for the thrill of release and crash, ripping into himself.
In *Barbed Hula*, Sigalit Landau spins a ring of knotted wire

around her naked waist, 59 long seconds of ripping flesh
while the sea behind her rocks fitfully toward and away

from the shore. She calls it an act of desensitization,
reality numbed by the force of exhilarating velocity.

15

A mile from the peak and much too high for piñon anymore,
a barking dog dissolves the spell—someone else on the trail.

From behind I watch Paul's calves pulse and pulse, the curves
of which still heat my thighs—sweet ache, want—like Peru

in 2004, snow flurries at the Pampacawana pass, the horses'
footing no better than ours, the moment he dismounted,

deciding to walk instead, watching his head, back, and legs
from up on horseback, knowing it was a singular moment

disappearing—ablation, downwasting, disarticulation.
We break into words—*Hey pup, beautiful lab, rattlesnake*

ahead—bits of sound almost bizarre in this alpine silence,
a half day from the city's habitual multiplicity, mornings

in the espresso line with the decidedly impatient, Gen X
and Gen Y in wireless earbuds, one saying, *I can't do it,*

I won't while texting, paying, sliding his phone deftly
into a pocket. At 12, Sierra attaches two photos

to a text of three words and a URL that takes me instantly
to the Alfred-Wegener Institute website: sounds

under the Antarctic ice shelf. And I believe we can do it,
follow the logical thread: power cord to outlet, outlet

to cables, cables through earth, earth to power station,
station to steam, steam from turbines, turbines stoked

by coal, coal from longwall mining machines, machines
with their spectacular drill bits going deep and deeper

into black rock, rock once a soupy peat—plant matter
and swamp crushed by 100 million years of pressure,

weight, and heat. Is this what the girl feels, down
into bone, wisps of hair riding the wind like cursive *m*'s?

How much do we want the deep?

Cocooned, he wrangles a green garden hose; she labors
to turn pages of a newspaper; sheets billow and waft

as the pillow dodges the sleeper's outstretched hand.
Lars Jan's *Holoscenes* traps humans in a tank of rising

water as a crowd in Times Square lifts a tide of cell phones,
beauty of bodies submerged in mundane tasks, as if

we could breathe in liquid, amphibious, as if lungs
could adapt this quickly to the shift from air to wet,

as if there is only a loveliness of bowl, chair, bucket
and not the anguish of so little space between surface

and glass—spasmic vocal cords, lungs bursting with water.

17

A month before the flood the sheep forgot to eat
and sleep, obsessively watched the stars at night,

told the shepherds the constellations foretold
the destruction of the world. The shepherds

gathered their flocks and pigs and families, climbed
the top of Ancasmarca, watched as the mountain

sank slowly into the sea. Sky, night and day, beheld
their long dizziness—the passing of sheep, herder,

pig, and kin. Six children survived as the mountain
lifted, and forever after the people minded the slightest

movement of stars, mapping and deducing and guessing.

18

In 2012 Dominique struggled at the end of day three.
Bobbe grew deliberate with her poles. My hips

went numb under my heavy pack. Later that night
in the tent I wrote, *No water from San Ysidro*

to the city limits, sweep of industrial waste—
tires, paint drums, cars upended and embedded

in earth. Mile 33 of 54, hiking the length
of a dying river, we lost the sense of our edges—

earlobes, fingernails, shins—more like stick figures
in the petroglyph in La Bajada Canyon, climbing

the ladder, disappearing into sun, wormhole
and moon. All was perforation.

19

Now deep in the aspens I tell Paul how I dream
their speckled trunks, leaves scattering flash—

at some point realize they are not trees, no,
I am standing between the legs of colossal birds,

looking upward into their massive underwings.
And I know a thunder below me will start

when they lift their anisodactyl feet, walk,
and I bounce up and tumble down fatally to earth.

The "Trembling Giant," Pando, weighs 6,615 tons,
spreads across 100 acres in Utah, 47,000 aspens

from a single seed, a single root system,
the world's heaviest organism. The stroke-sensitive

neuron MrgprB4+ explains why mice respond
positively to petting. The female katydid

has humanlike ears on its legs, tympanums vibrating
at the frequencies of their male counterparts.

The wingspan of the female Atlas moth can reach
a foot with a surface area of 62 square inches.

It has no mouth, lives only 14 days after wriggling
from its cocoon, sprouting enormous maplike wings.

Have we ever thought to count these out?
I mean, count?

20

At the Biscayne National Park welcome center
I arrive too late for a snorkeling trip, refuse the self-

guided tour, exit the building chiding myself. I watch
the boat crowded with snorkelers, little black dots

receding quickly into the distance. When we were little
the blue bathtub was big as a lagoon, and we'd take turns

being *bridge* and *diver*, holding our noses, swimming
end to end, pretending we were Jacques Cousteau,

saying, *I saw a whale, an eel, a sea horse, a starfish*,
plunging again and again until forced to get out,

make room for two more. I'd delay and linger, dive
once more to hold on: dreamy waterlog. At Xel-Há,

Quintana Roo, 1996, numb to my severely sunburned
back, I swam with the magnificents: *Pterophyllum*,

Paracanthurus hepatus, *Sphyraena*, tried to stay submerged
all the way back to the airport—saltwater blurring eyes

and earshot. I'd become something else. Like the infants
in that swimming pool footage, deep under the surface,

chubby thighs and forearms, pupils half-focused, belonging
to some other world of echo and gills. Relenting, I reenter

the building, wander to the back where dioramas display
creatures so fantastical—fingerprint cyphoma, rainbow

wrasse—I feel an opening, wide, imagine Spider Woman
and the clans actually listen to Sotuknang, abandon

the assault on ice and mountain, walk away
from the back door to the Fourth World.

21

At the crest we find a rocky perch to eat sandwiches,
share a leftover slice of chocolate cake, anticipate

the long bath after the descent, kneesache, therapeutic
heat, sheen on Paul's neck and back as I lather

and sponge them off, lean in, seam of bathwater
between us, Siamese, counting 1, 2, 3, 4, 5, 6, 7, 8,

9, 10, 11, 12, 13, 14 for all the years and stitchings,
our bodies, other bodies intersecting—shoreline,

horizon—Alexandra all those years ago, mixing
dirt and water in a pie tin, her small hands, giddy

screams, *What I made, what I made*,
tipping the slop on Niall's small head.

22

Watching *Chasing Ice* I waver between wonder, grief,
urgency. Balog undergoes a fourth surgery, unwraps

his swollen knees in the tent, sleeps, descends again
into the crevice, defying doctor's wishes. Ice, aperture,

images of water-carved blue almost make me forget
his refraying tendons, carbon heat making water flow.

How far is the distance between us—me, Río, Peter,
his young assistants? They camp on the precipice,

wait, and nearly give up when the glacier starts to quake
and crack, ice the size of Manhattan calving into the sea.

How old are they? How much does it weigh to be 25
years in the world at this fateful witnessing?

23

The Mixtec believe Man committed a grievous fault,
precipitating the great deluge, and one afternoon

at Hallandale Beach I went too far out, beyond the buoy,
ignoring the lifeguard's shrill whistles with a thrill

of defiance, as if no one knew better than me how much
my body can do, and I resented whatever boundary

that just-past-high-school upstart set, arbitrary,
for somebody else, and besides I felt a strange

exhilarating lightness from collarbone to pelvis,
as if some cosmic ether was bottled up miraculously

in me, the chosen, yes—and then a thunder
under me bumped my left heel. Panicked,

I swam frantically back to shore.

24

The descent from 10,300 to 7,000 feet is quicker, hard
on the knees and thighs, ache in the neck. In 2 days,

extreme drought will close the trail with the Jemez Fire,
Pecos Fire, Black Forest Fire ablaze, on the same day

62 million in the Midwest prepare for a 100-year storm,
the same day orange signs go up along the Bosque Trail,

EXTREME FIRE DANGER, EXTREME FIRE DANGER,
the same day the governor shuts down the Rio Grande

watershed in three counties, the same afternoon I cycle
south from the BioPark along the Barr Canal, where

the desert cottontail race me for short distances, where
the skunk family crosses, crowds the burrow, disappears,

where beavers leave their marks on pointed stumps of trees,
where the trail unfolds from small farms to industrial flatland

along the concrete diversion channel, where a few wan trees
hum *see* and *see*. The lone survivor of the Yarnell Hill Fire

fled his lookout post as the wind whipped the flames
and they suddenly changed direction. The blaze torched

his perch, chased the other 19 Granite Mountain Hotshots
into a valley—the worst place, where the only choice

was to wriggle into their silver, podlike heat bags and pray
as the fire roared through, taking them all. And the one

just a short distance away. All he could do: watch.

25

In 2013, 33 young Indo-Pacific bottlenose dolphins
washed up dead on the beaches of Gulph St. Vincent.

Immunosuppressed by heat stress, they succumbed
quickly to the morbillivirus, transmitting it to others

in their close-knit pods. And so I force the image,
make the girl at the shore turn and unlock herself,

climb the sand up and away from the sea to the comfort
of porch, socks, yellow kitchen. A ruse, palliation.

26

To the left of the trail we spot the little nipple cactus,
Mammillaria meiacantha, tiny labyrinthine bowl ringed

with white flowers. It grows and thrives between rocks,
up and through asphalt cracks, with only a few drops

of water. Boil the pulp, apply the mush for an earache.
On the map I see we are too far north for this variety

but I think I'm right—elongated and scarlet fruit, golden
anthers, now hot and dry enough at this elevation

to take root. The black and yellow *Atelopus zeteki*,
Panamanian golden frog, communicates via semaphore,

waving at rivals and prospective mates. Ancient lore
held that in death it turned to gold. Even one sighting

predicts good fortune. Once saved from extinction-
by-poaching, *zeteki* now survives only in captivity—

rising heat in the mountains spurs evaporation, prompts
cloud formation, decreases daytime temps, raises

nighttime highs, igniting the deadly chytrid fungus,
thickening its delicate skin, triggering cardiac arrest.

Ophiopogon japonicus, also called mondo grass,
needs no fertilizer, is rarely affected by disease,

adjusts deftly to changes in water conditions. Admired
for its tenaciousness, *Ophiopogon* now shows signs

of decreasing resilience, approaching a threshold
at which it cannot survive. *Acropora cervicornis*,

staghorn coral, yields compounds that treat leukemia,
tumors, heart disease, and asthma. Vulnerable

to bleaching, its population has plummeted 80%
over the past 30 years. The International Union

for Conservation of Nature has declared its status:
critically endangered.

28

For three consecutive nights I dream we are stick figures
in a giant earth tome: book of mudslides, book of super-

storms, book of drought-devastated fields inside which
we tumble like the drawings at Puako—right side up,

sideways, flipped. Are we singing? Are we dancing?
Are we waving frantically in distress?

29

On simultaneous screens, Kimsooja's Needle Woman
stands motionless in the throngs of Delhi, Lagos, Tokyo,

Shanghai, Mexico City, London, New York, Cairo.
Filmed from the back, it's the absolute stillness of her head,

shoulders, black braid. Crowds move toward, around,
and past. It must take everything to hold her place

in the chaos. And I want it—still, stillness. Make it stop.

30

The Selk'nam believe a long time ago people did not die
but grew so tired of being human they willed themselves

into a long and fitful sleep in which they were transformed
into creatures, rocks, clouds, and trees. After many hundred

years they woke to find themselves strange, and refreshed.

31

The late Robert M. Carter, James Cook University, notable
climate change skeptic, offered "Global Warming: Ten Facts

and Ten Myths on Climate Change," a platform for arguing
against a tidal wave of warnings. *Ecosystems have adapted*

*to changes in climate since time immemorial. The result
is a process called evolution. Mankind can and does adapt*

to all climate extremes. So I turn to his video lectures as if
I too am a skeptic, an effort to understand who I am not,

someone so different she seems a member of an alien race—
bright winged, prescient. I maintain my skeptical stance

for almost two hours, log off, switch to news of hurricanes,
wildfires, extratropical cyclones. But, for a short time,

I did feel certainty. The earth is old and changeable.
Nature's cycles are long. This too will pass, and children

will continue to produce children who birth
their own, and so forth and so on.

32

At the dinner table Little J. R. recites Genesis 1:26.
At seven he is remarkably fluent in the memorization

of Bible verses. His evangelical school and church
offer him supreme confidence in the sovereignty

of the human race. He asks, *Auntie, why all these
maps and books and photos of frogs on your desk?*

He listens earnestly as I explain, places his small arm
around me, tells me not to worry: *God will take care of it.*

33

Anyway, the girl never really turns to me, never
shows her inscrutable face, and it's the smallness

in her elbow, something delicate about her calves,
and I know I'm supposed to know what ankle,

cotton, dark hair signify in this amalgamation—
a pictogram I study even while sleeping for every

detail of cloud, breaker, and sleeve. Her bones
are still young enough to ache at night, lengthening,

growing denser by the hour.

34

Hiking down a mountain is double charged—relief
with some measure of grief. Below, the city unfolds

in squares and streaks, crush of trees at the Rio Grande,
mesa extending endlessly to the west. From this distance

green and brown are wedded in repeating patterns
of settlement (where the water is) and wandering (away

from the river), the freedom we've enjoyed for so long,
engineering and infrastructure built on a firm belief

in everlasting resources. On Baffin Island, Arctic
Archipelago, Briner and his fellow paleoclimatologists

drill through ice and sediment. Tubes of Holocenian mud
serve as remarkably accurate climate analogues, telling

the future of ours: temperature increase now exceeds
all variations of the past 1,000 years.

35

According to the Wintun, people came into existence late,
devoured water and land at an alarming rate. One man

dreamed a whirlwind; the others knew this was a bad sign.
They fled to an earth lodge as the winds started up, downing

the trees. The dreamer remained outside, pressed against
a post, describing what was coming: thundering rain.

Footpaths, fields, houses were swept away, but the dreamer
held tight, telling his people the story of water. Finally

the earth lodge lifted, and the post and the dreamer too,
and nothing was left but a tide over the earth.

Bobbe, Dominique, and I tell our story to a fifth grade class,
the year we hiked 54 miles, wet and dry, from 11,000 feet

to the Santa Fe River's confluence with the Rio Grande,
so they connect the water they wash with, pee in, drink

with the lush upper watershed as well as the desolation
unfolding downstream. Try for a delicate balance of beauty—

willows, beaver dams—and warning—salt cedar, extreme
incision, pharmaceutical effluent. They sit at the edges

of six tables, end to end, on either side of one long river-
blue ribbon of curved paper, painting native trees, river stones,

water creatures. A girl raises her hand, asks, *How old are you,
how much water do you waste at home, and your kids*

*and your dogs too, and who took care of your husbands
while you were gone, living on the river all that time?*

forcing a spin of dizzying prioritizing: third-, second-, first-
level concerns measured by sand slipping quickly

from the upper bulb of the hourglass.

37

Before I leave Miami for good I take the long ride
out to Key Biscayne for the lift of two bridges—

two high points between the Keys where the road
seems to disappear and bicycle and I float over the bay.

In the landlocked west something similar happens
on the descent toward the White House Ruins

in Canyon de Chelly—the trail narrow, the drop deep
enough to frighten, line of the rim above a ragged

circle if you spin slowly around. Both sensations
spell *ancient*, and beyond it and the abandoned

cliff dwellings, deserted caves, empty mansions
under the sea are simply versions of a repeating

story, and I can let go of the girl and the effort,
Professor Wanless can you blame us, we've had

our short time—brilliant and careless—
much will remain after our disappearance.

38

In the next 35 years, 400 million climate migrants will flee
coastlines and inland flooding, abandoning to water

most of what they have in a strange, reverse narrative,
like the girl on the shore stepping back from the waves

as if caught on old VHS tapes when the ribbon gets stuck—
forward, snapping back, forward and snap—and so

we fixate on the corner of her white hem as it keeps making
a perfect loop, O O O O, like the hot white trail of a sparkler,

the mesmerized look on Annelisa's face as we taught her
how to keep the stick circling in the dark till she sees it:

the white continuous line, and when it burned too close
to her fingers the way she yelped, bolted to the nearest body

of water, wine in the plastic cup of her grandmother,
arc of the spark line from stick to liquid—the panic,

the way my mother stretched the cup forward
while leaning back—the sizzle of the spark

as it broke the surface.

39

Hiking into the transition zone, the juniper gives way
to ponderosa pine, Gambel oak, New Mexico locust.

Vertigo takes me down, over a fallen trunk.
Paul crouches, drops his pack, checks for blood, waits

for the spinning to stop, one of too many episodes—
11 years battling with what no doctor can explain:

inconclusive ear tests, no vestibular neuritis, negative
brain scans, scant exposure to mercury, lead, and tin.

Articles about benign paroxysmal positional vertigo
theorize that calcium crystals break off the utricle,

tumble into the cupula—the degenerative effects of stress,
aging, or some other trauma. Zsuzsanna Szegedi

paints trees from upside-down perspectives, as if
we are headstanding, looking upward into pleaches,

roots pooling at eye level. From there the canopy balloons
into a new thing, sea green, gift of sick reorientation.

40

The last half mile of the descent is tough on the back
and so I begin to count my steps, a distraction

that creates a soothing beat in my head. I count in threes
and nines, lucky numbers, insert the names of insects

and plants, first and second cousins, rivers and bays,
until the girl finally turns to me and waves, split-

second recognition, and I can almost leave her
fearlessly on the shore. In Paris's 10ème arrondissement

Basia Irland launches *Book XIV* on the Canal St. Martin,
an ice book embedded with native seeds, ecolanguage,

riparian text. It liquefies as it floats, reseeding
the riverbank. The toddler on her website sits

cross-legged before an ice book, small, dark head
and purplish dress, patterns of seeds the story

she reads, palms up, hands cupped, as if divining.

41

The Yellowstone believe at one time the People hunted
for sport, burned and cleared forests, stopped thinking

of animals as their kin. And so Great Spirit let the smoke
from their fires sit in the valley. They coughed and choked

but did not abandon their ways. Great Spirit sent thunder
and rain, flooding roads and dwellings, inundating the fields.

Only then did they turn to Spotted Bear, medicine man,
who sent the youngest hunters for Buffalo. For weeks

they slogged and searched. Along the way fear forced them
to transform their relationship with nature. They returned

with the hide of a white bull who drowned in the floodwaters.
Half-starved, the People watched as Spotted Bear scraped

and stretched the hide for hours and days until it grew the size
of the whole of the valley. They lifted it and huddled beneath.

Finally, the rains stopped and the sun emerged, shining
hour after hour, day after day, shrinking the hide until

all that was left was a patch that dissolved into a rainbow
arch. And Spotted Bear declared that the People,

no longer at odds with the earth, would survive.

42

In 2013, hundreds of Miamians walked and chalked
26 miles of city streets—a high waterline where,

by century's end, three feet of sea level rise will remake
the city into somewhere more like Venice, Jakarta,

ancient Alexandria. For over 15,000 years pilgrims
have hiked the circular path beneath Mount Kailash—

52 kilometers, 52,000 meters, 2,047,244 inches.
Ascending the peak at 21,778 feet is forbidden.

Some complete the journey in 25,000 prostrations.
At first each rustle, footfall, birdsong is precise.

One can detail their singularities, contours, length.
Then a blur comes on, defying separation, until

one song rings through the body, mountain, air,
and all breath seems one harmonic respiration.

Pilgrims believe making the pass at Dolma La
and all the way back will erase the sins of a lifetime.

43

The adolescent goddess Hadanishté was encircled
by creatures—thin, delirious—reflected in the tears

of her people. She punished the tribe for negligence,
put them to work reassembling the fragments

of a disintegrating world. After much toil each piece—
cleaned and burnished—flashed a sliver of sunlight

by day, moonlight by night, billions of which could not
be looked at directly. In this way they learned

to be reverent and disciplined, to live on the edge
of great balance—the sum of incalculable beauty.

NOTES

8: Bill Viola, *The Raft*, 2004, large-scale video/sound installation, viewed February 3, 2012, in the exhibition *Bill Viola: Liber Insularum*, Museum of Contemporary Art, North Miami.

9: E. A. Wallis Budge, *The Project Gutenberg eBook of the Book of the Dead*, Project Gutenberg, accessed May 5, 2014, https://www.gutenberg.org/files/7145/7145-h/7145-h.htm.

14: Sigalit Landau, *Barbed Hula*, 2001, video installation, viewed September 2015 at the Centre Pompidou, Paris. Quote is from the text panel accompanying the video.

16: Lars Jan and Early Morning Opera, *Holoscenes*, 2017, installation and performances for the World Science Festival, Times Square, New York City, accessed April 22, 2020, http://arts.timessquarenyc.org/times-square-arts/projects/at-the-crossroads/holoscenes/index.aspx.

18: Bobbe Besold, Valerie Martínez, and Dominique Mazeaud, *Rivers Run Through Us*, 2012, ecowalk of the length of the endangered Santa Fe River, Santa Fe, New Mexico, http://www.riversrunthroughus.org.

19: Breanna Draxler, "Brain Basis for Why Petting Feels Good," *Discover*, January 31, 2013, accessed May 2013, https://www.discovermagazine.com/mind/brain-basis-for-why-petting-feels-good.

22: Jeff Orlowski, director, *Chasing Ice* (New York: Submarine Delux Films, 2012), documentary.

29: Kimsooja, *A Needle Woman*, 1999–2001, multichannel video installation, viewed at the Miami Art Museum, August 12, 2012.

31: John Cook, "Climate Misinformation by Source: Bob Carter." *Skeptical Science* (blog), accessed January 19, 2019, https://www.skepticalscience.com/Bob_Carter_arg.htm.

34: Ellen Goldbaum, "Deep in Arctic Mud, Geologists Find Strong Evidence of Climate Change," State University of New York at Buffalo, news release, January 18, 2007, accessed May 28, 2013, https://www.buffalo.edu/news/releases/2007/01/8365.html.

39: Zsuzsanna Szegedi, *Awkward Beauty*, 1999–2009, https://www.zsuzsanna.com/AwkwardBeauty.html.

40: Basia Irland, *Ice Books: Ice Receding/Books Reseeding*, 2007–2017, Basia Irland's website, accessed November 12, 2014, http://www.basiairland.com.

42: Eve Mosher, *HighWaterLine/Miami*, 2013, https://www.evemosher.com/highwaterline#/highwaterline-miami/.

43: *Hadanisht'é*, in colloquial Navajo, means "to be entire," "to be whole," "to be *all there*."

ABOUT THE AUTHOR

Valerie Martínez received her MFA in poetry from the University of Arizona in 1989. She has published several books of poetry, including *Absence Luminescent* (Four Way Books, 1999), winner of the Levis Prize in Poetry and a Greenwall Fund grant from the Academy of American Poets; *World to World* (University of Arizona Press, 2004); *Each and Her* (University of Arizona Press, 2010), winner of the Arizona Book Award and Honorable Mention in the International Latino Book Awards; and *This Is How It Began* (Press of the Palace of the Governors, 2010). Her poems have appeared widely in journals, media outlets, and anthologies, including *The Best American Poetry*, the *Washington Post*, *American Poetry: Next Generation*, and *Touching the Fire: Fifteen Poets of Today's Latino Renaissance*. Martínez has previously taught at the Universities of Arizona, New Mexico, and Miami, Ursinus College, College of Santa Fe, New Mexico Highlands University, and the Institute of American Indian Arts. She was poet laureate of Santa Fe, New Mexico, from 2008 to 2010.